DATE DUE

ANIMAL PREY

Octopuses

SANDRA MARKLE

LERNER PUBLICATIONS COMPANY / MINNEAPOLIS

THE ANIMAL WORLD
IS FULL OF
PREY.

Prey are the animals that predators eat. Predators must find, catch, kill, and eat other animals in order to survive. But prey animals aren't always easy to catch or kill. Some have eyes on the sides of their heads to let them see predators coming from all directions. Some are colored to blend in and hide. Some prey are built to run, leap, fly, or swim fast to get away. And still others sting, bite, or use chemicals to defend themselves. Octopuses live in shallow coral reefs and the oceans' cold dark depths. *They are all equipped to defend themselves against their enemies. This southern star-eyed octopus can hide in plain sight.*

It's a summer evening in southern California. A pale twilight glow filters all the way to the sea bottom. There, in her den among a tumble of rocks, a giant Pacific octopus is at home. She is ready to search for a meal. Octopuses are predators. But they are also prey for ocean animals such as sharks, seals, and dolphins.

First, the female octopus looks out to check for enemies lurking nearby. Then she pokes out her eight long arms, called tentacles. The two rows of ringlike suckers on each tentacle are loaded with sensors. The suckers help her grip surfaces. The sensors allow her to feel water currents and taste the chemical signals that could mean a predator is nearby.

Sensing no danger, she crawls out of her den. She tightens some of her muscles to draw water through a slit into her sacklike body. Her body doesn't have a hard skeleton, so it swells like a balloon with the water. Then by tightening, or contracting, other muscles, she forces the water out through her funnel. She can aim her hoselike funnel in any direction.

She lifts her tentacles so the water can hold up her body. Then she aims the water to shoot out behind her. This propels her forward.

The giant octopus has two large eyes and can see very well. As she swims, she keeps watch. Even when the female stops to rest, she looks around for prey and predators.

Puffs of sandy gravel drift up like a dust cloud. They alert the octopus to a crab shuffling across the seafloor. The octopus spreads her tentacles like a net and drops down, enveloping the crab as she lands. Her suckers taste her catch. This way, she makes sure it's something she wants to eat.

The crab struggles, but the female octopus anchors her catch with her suckers. Next, she drills a hole in the crab's shell with her radula, a tooth-studded tongue. Then she uses her radula to inject her saliva into the crab. The saliva of most octopuses contains venom (poison) that paralyzes its prey. Once the crab had stopped struggling, the giant Pacific octopus will use her tentacles to carry it to her den. There, safely tucked away from hunting predators, she will pull the flesh from the crab and toss the shell onto the garbage pile outside her den.

On her way home with her catch, the octopus spots a seal. This hungry predator, searching for a meal of its own, is swimming straight toward her.

The octopus drops the crab, draws water into her body sac, and quickly contracts her muscles. Blasting water out, she quickly jets away. But she is only out of range of the seal for a moment. The predator is still after her.

Octopuses are nature's escape artists, and it's time for the octopus to use another of her tricks. She squirts out a blast of ink. An octopus's ink is a mixture of a dark-colored fluid and mucus. It is produced and stored in the ink sac near the end of the animal's digestive system. When she's ready to squirt the ink, the female octopus's brain signals the ink sac to dump the ink into the end of her digestive tube. Then the next jet of water blasts the ink out. The dark fluid sticks to the mucus droplets, creating a dense, dark cloud that holds together in a thick blob. By the time the seal checks out the ink blob, the giant Pacific octopus has disappeared.

The octopus hasn't actually disappeared. She dropped to the seafloor, where she blends in with her surroundings. The octopus's skin is covered with special color cells called chromatophores. Each chromatophore is like a paint-filled balloon surrounded by muscles. When the muscles relax, the colored sac remains small. But when they contract, the color-filled sac expands. The octopus's brain coordinates which sacs remain small and which sacs expand, creating an effect that makes her blend in with her surroundings. To add to her disguise, the octopus's muscles push up flaps to form bumps on her usually smooth skin.

The giant Pacific octopus is
good at changing its appearance.
But the mimic octopus of Indonesia is the
master of this art. In the coral reefs where it lives, the mimic octopus
changes its body shape to resemble something a predator would not attack.
For example, it might shape its tentacles and body to look like a stingray,
complete with a long, sting-tipped tail.

Or it may put six tentacles down a hole and stretch out its other two tentacles in a way that makes it look like a banded, venomous sea snake.

The southern keeled octopus lives in shallow waters off the coasts of Australia and New Zealand. This octopus uses a different method to disappear from predators. It buries itself.

The octopus digs its tentacles deep into the sand and pulls its body down over them. Once buried, the animal pokes out one or both of its big eyes. Then it stays still and keeps watch until the predator moves on and the coast is clear.

The blue-ringed octopus lives in warm, shallow waters from Australia to Japan. It doesn't try to escape or hide from predators. Its skin turns bright yellow and black. Vivid blue rings make sure the octopus gets noticed. This octopus is small—its tentacle span is smaller than a child's hand. But its saliva packs a poisonous punch. The bright colors are an alarm telling predators to stay away.

Like other octopuses, the saliva of the blue-ringed has a paralyzing chemical. The prey of the blue-ringed is often a crab that is bigger than it is, so the chemical in its saliva has to be very strong. In fact, some humans have died after being bitten by these small octopuses.

The blue-ringed octopus uses its coloring to warn predators. But the octopus wants to go unnoticed while stalking its own prey. When hunting, it changes its skin color to blend in with its surroundings.

The banded string-arm octopus also lives in the warm coastal waters of Australia. It has another special way to escape predators. When a banded string-arm is attacked, it sheds one or more of its eight long tentacles. Each tentacle has a weak section near the body where it can snap off. The octopus's tentacles have many nerves that control movement, so a shed tentacle continues to wiggle. The suckers even suck when the predator attacks. While the predator overpowers and munches on the discarded tentacle, the octopus has time to swim to safety.

The tentacle isn't lost forever, though. A new tentacle grows back in about six weeks.

Most octopuses live on the seafloor. But the glass octopus spends its whole life in mid-water. This is the part of the ocean between the surface and the bottom. With a tentacle spread only about as wide as a dinner plate, a glass octopus is a bite-sized treat for fishes, small sharks, squids, and seals. Luckily, the glass octopus has a special defense that enables it to avoid predators. This octopus is transparent. And its brain, eyes, and digestive gland—its main solid parts—are so small that they are hard for a predator to see. The female even produces transparent eggs. To keep the developing young safe, the female carries her brood along with her, tucked inside the closed umbrella of her tentacles.

When the female giant Pacific octopus is about three years old, she mates and lays her eggs—nearly one hundred thousand of them. The eggs are no bigger than rice grains. The female lays them stuck together in long clusters. Then she uses her tentacles to attach these clusters to the ceiling and walls of her nursery den. From then on, she never leaves her developing young. She stays on guard, prepared to attack any fish, eel, or crab that tries to sneak into the den to eat her eggs.

She cares for her brood by blowing oxygen-rich water from her funnel onto the eggs. Oxygen in the water passes through the soft egg cases to the developing young inside. They need oxygen to live and grow. The female also often strokes the egg clusters. She uses her suckers to clean away any bacteria or algae that might be growing on them.

The baby giant Pacific octopuses develop for nearly six months. They live on the yolk (the stored food supply) inside their eggs. When the babies are ready to hatch, their mother blows forcefully on the eggs and bumps them roughly with her tentacles. This helps break open the egg cases. Without any help, the babies immediately jet through the water, swimming up toward the surface of the ocean. Along the way, fish, squid, and jellyfish eat many of them.

The babies that survive float among plankton, tiny microscopic animals that live near the surface of the water. The plankton layer is also a nursery for baby crabs, jellyfish, and other sea animals. The baby octopuses eat anything they can catch and overpower. And they try to avoid being caught and eaten by other predators.

The mother giant Pacific octopus hasn't eaten during all the months that she's been guarding and caring for her developing babies. After her brood has left the den, the mother crawls out and soon dies. Sunflower sea stars discover her body. Bit by bit, the sea stars eat most of the dead octopus. Crabs finish off the scraps they leave. These animals are scavengers, part of the ocean floor's cleanup crew.

In a few weeks, the baby octopuses are about as big as the thumb of an adult human. Then they return to the seafloor. Predators like this cup coral catch and eat many of the young octopuses. But those that become experts at using their natural hide-and-escape abilities survive.

The young octopuses that survive also develop their ability to stalk and catch small crabs and other prey. Sometimes they eat dead animals, like this dogfish shark. All kinds of food energy help the young octopuses grow into their full giant size.

These male and female giant Pacific octopuses are about three years old. They are ready to reproduce. The female is bigger than the male. She needs a large body to hold all the eggs she will produce. The male uses one of his tentacles to transfer a packet of sperm, or male reproductive cells, into the female's body. She may store the sperm for months before she's ready to produce eggs and care for them.

Most mother octopuses care for their eggs in dens. Some, such as the glass octopus and this blue-ringed octopus, carry their eggs along with them. All mother octopuses watch over their eggs and try to protect the developing young from predators until the young hatch. Then another generation of octopuses will join the cycle of life, a constant struggle to survive between predators and prey.

Looking Back

- Look closely at the southern star-eyed octopus on page 3. See how it is using the suckers on its tentacles to grip the ground and pull itself across the seafloor.

- Look back at the octopus in its den on page 5. What makes that tight space a good resting place?

- Look again at the octopuses in the book, and notice the ways they take advantage of not having a bony skeleton. Imagine how differently you might move if you lacked a hard skeleton.

- Compare the baby giant Pacific octopus on page 30 with the adult on page 35. In what ways is the baby like the adult? In what ways is it different?

Glossary

ALGAE: tiny plants, mostly too small to see without a microscope

BACTERIA: tiny one-celled organisms that sometimes cause diseases

CHROMATOPHORE: a cell that contains color pigment that changes the octopus's skin color

EGG: the female reproductive cell, which will develop into a baby octopus

FUNNEL: the body part that expels water to jet the octopus from one place to another. Ink, waste products, the female's eggs, and the male's sperm are also expelled through the funnel.

INK: a dark liquid produced and stored in a special sac and ejected through the funnel to confuse predators

PLANKTON: tiny plants and animals that float on the surface of water

PREDATOR: an animal that hunts and eats other animals in order to survive

PREY: an animal that a predator catches to eat

RADULA: a tonguelike part of the octopus that is studded with teeth

SCAVENGER: an animal that feeds on dead animals

SPERM: the male reproductive cell. When the sperm joins with the female's egg, a baby octopus develops.

SUCKER: a cup-shaped structure on an octopus's tentacle that creates suction to hold prey, help the octopus crawl, and to defend against predators. Suckers also have touch and taste sensors.

TENTACLE: one of an octopus's eight muscular, flexible parts used for movement, capturing food, and during reproduction

Further Information

Books

Cerullo, Mary M. *The Octopus: Phantom of the Sea.* New York: Dutton, 1997. This is an introduction to the behavior and intelligence of the octopus.

Wallace, Karen. *Gentle Giant Octopus.* Cambridge, MA: Candlewick Press, 2002. This book for young readers describes the life of a female giant octopus as she finds food, escapes predators, and then cares for her eggs until they hatch.

Videos

The Fascinating Underwater World of Octopus: Giant of the Deep. Walnut Creek, CA: Diamond Entertainment, 2003. This film is a real-life drama about an octopus's life.

The Under Sea World of Jacques Cousteau/Octopus Los Angeles: Universal Studios, 1989. This film examines the octopus in its ocean world.

Websites

Exciting Cephalopods
http://www.earlham.edu/~merkeka/exciting_cephalopods.htm
Find out more about octopuses and their closest relatives.

Giant Pacific Octopus Exhibit
http://www.mbayaq.org/efc/octopus.asp
Take a virtual tour of the giant Pacific octopus exhibit at the Monterey Bay Aquarium. Don't miss the video of feeding time.

Index

With love, for Don and Trish Ferguson

The author would like to thank the following people for sharing their expertise and enthusiasm: Dr. Mark Norman, Curator of Molluscs, Museum of Victoria, Australia; Dr. Clyde Roper, Department of Invertebrate Zoology, National Museum of Natural History, Smithsonian Institution, Washington, D.C.; and Dr. David Scheele, Marine Biologist with Environmental Science Department, Alaska Pacific University, Anchorage, Alaska. The author would also like to express a special thank-you to Skip Jeffery for his help and support during the creative process.

Photo Acknowledgments

The images in this book are used with the permission of: © Fred Bavendam, pp. 1, 5, 7, 9, 10, 29, 30, 35, 36; © Mark Norman, pp. 3, 23, 24, 25; © Jeffrey L. Rotman/CORBIS, pp. 6, 13, 34; © Rodger Jackman/Oxford Scientific Films/Jupiter Images, p. 8; © Brandon D. Cole/CORBIS, p. 12; © Fred Bavendam/Minden Pictures, p. 14; © Bob Cranston/SeaPics.com, p. 17; © Roger Steene, pp. 18, 19; © John C. Lewis/SeaPics.com, pp. 20, 21; © Ron & Valerie Taylor/SeaPics.com, p. 22; © Richard E. Young, p. 27; © Stuart Westmorland/CORBIS, p. 33; © David Hall/SeaPics.com, p. 37.
Cover: © Rodger Jackman/Oxford Scientific Films/Jupiter Images.

Lerner Publications Company
A division of Lerner Publishing Group
241 First Avenue North
Minneapolis, MN 55401

Website address: www.lernerbooks.com

Library of Congress Cataloging-in-Publication Data

Markle, Sandra.
    Octopuses / by Sandra Markle.
      p.   cm. — (Animal prey)
    Includes bibliographical references and index.
    ISBN-13: 978–0–8225–6063–0 (lib. bdg. : alk. paper)
    ISBN-10: 0–8225–6063–1 (lib. bdg. : alk. paper)
    1. Octopuses—Juvenile literature. I. Title.
QL430.3.O2M373 2007
594'.56—dc22   2005036350

Manufactured in the United States of America
1 2 3 4 5 6 – DP – 12 11 10 09 08 07